Writing and Language Handbook

Grade 1

**Macmillan
McGraw-Hill**

New York   Farmington

Macmillan/McGraw-Hill

A Division of The **McGraw-Hill** Companies

Copyright © 1997 Macmillan/McGraw-Hill, a Division of the Educational and Professional Publishing Group of The McGraw-Hill Companies, Inc.

Editorial Development: Hudson Publishing Associates

Macmillan/McGraw-Hill
1221 Avenue of the Americas
New York, New York 10020

Printed in the United States of America.

ISBN 0-02-181655-7 / 1
5 6 7 8 9 POH 02 01 00 99 98

PART 1: WRITING 4

The Writing Process 6
Types of Writing 9
Purposes for Writing 13
Writer's Journal 14
Listening and Speaking 16

PART 2: STUDY SKILLS
AND LANGUAGE SKILLS 18

Study Skills

Dictionary 20
Parts of a Book 21
Calendar 22
Telephone Directory 23
Directions 24
Lists 25
Diagrams 26
Charts and Graphs 27
Maps 28
Schedules 29
Labels 30
Messages 31

Language Skills

Punctuation Guide 32
Capitalization Guide 34

Spelling and Vocabulary 35

PART 3: WRITING MODELS 38

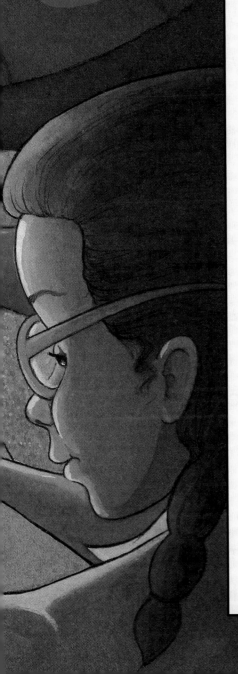

PART ONE

Writing

CONTENTS

The Writing Process

Prewriting and Drafting 6
Revising and Editing 7
Publishing and Reflecting 8

Types of Writing

Descriptive Writing 9
Narrative Writing 10
Informative Writing 11
Expository Writing 12

Purposes for Writing 13

Writer's Journal 14

Listening and Speaking 16

THE
WRITING PROCESS

PREWRITING

When you write, you save your words. You can read them again and again. Other people can read them, too.

You can write about anything you like. Write about something that happened, about a person, or about your favorite thing to eat. Before you write, list your ideas.

DRAFTING

When you start to write, don't worry about making mistakes. Just be sure to get your ideas onto the paper.

REVISING AND EDITING

Always look back at your writing.
Do you want to add another word?
Do you want to change how a word
is spelled? Now is the time to do it.

more **INFO**

Page 35 has some spelling hints for you.

7

PUBLISHING

When you are ready, show your writing to your friends and family.

You might put your writing on a bulletin board in school. You might hang it in your home where your family can see it.

REFLECTING

Read your own words again. Does your writing tell exactly what you want it to? Think about how to make your writing better next time.

I like noodles. They are slurpy! My friends share them, too. That makes eating them even more fun!

TYPES OF WRITING

DESCRIPTIVE WRITING

Writing can do many things. Writing that describes tells how something looks, smells, tastes, feels, or sounds.

These socks are long and red. Do you think they are smelly, too? If they are, you can describe that to your readers.

NARRATIVE WRITING

CHECK it OUT!

✔ *Look at a story you wrote. Does it have a beginning, a middle, and an end?*

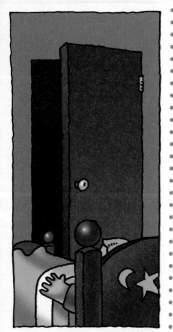

Some writing tells a story.

The storm shook the house. It shook Jack's bed. He woke up. He saw the closet door open very, very slowly.

After this story beginning, the writer will tell what happens next. Then the writer will finish by telling what happens at the end of the story.

When you write a story or tell about something that you have seen or done, tell what happened in **time order.** Then your readers will be able to follow along easily.

INFORMATIVE WRITING

What's new? You can read an article to find out about what is happening in the world around you. This is one kind of informative writing.

Writing that informs gives facts and details about a topic. It tells *who, what, when, where,* and *why.*

You might use a chart or a diagram with this kind of writing. This can help make the information clearer for your readers.

PSST!

A report or a letter can give information, too.

Shuttle Lifts Off Today in Florida

Cabin

Cargo Bay

11

EXPOSITORY WRITING

When you get back from soccer practice, you feel hot! A frozen juice pop would be perfect. But how do you make them? A recipe would tell you exactly what to do.

Expository writing—writing that explains—tells how to do or make something. This kind of writing usually has steps to follow in a special order. Sometimes the steps are numbered. That makes it extra easy!

keep in mind

When you do how-to writing, be sure your steps are in the correct order.

GRAPE JUICE

ORANGE JUICE

PINEAPPLE JUICE

PURPOSES FOR WRITING

Why is writing important? Do some detective work to find out!

WRITER'S JOURNAL

A journal is like a photo album. But instead of pictures, you save words. Did something make you laugh? Did you meet a new friend? Write about it in your journal.

You can use a notebook as a journal. Some writers use pieces of

paper and keep them in a journal folder. All writers try to write in their journals every day.

You can write about anything you want in your journal. And you don't have to share it with anyone— unless you want to.

CHECK *it* **OUT!**

A journal is a good place to keep:
▶ *thoughts and ideas for writing*
▶ *new words*
▶ *words that are hard to spell*
You can draw pictures in your journal, too.

15

LISTENING AND SPEAKING

HELPFUL PARTNERS

Listen to your partner. You may get some good tips.

▶ Try to listen without interrupting.

▶ Try not to get upset. Remember, your partner is trying to help you.

When you speak to your partner:

▶ Try to say something nice.

▶ Say <u>why</u> you didn't like something, to help your partner make it better the next time.

GROUPS ARE PARTNERS, TOO!

You can share your writing with more than one person. That can be good, too—except when everyone talks at once!

How can you be a helpful partner in a group?

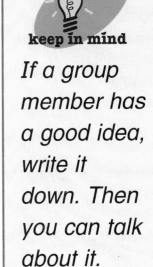

keep in mind

If a group member has a good idea, write it down. Then you can talk about it.

▶ Let everyone have a turn.

▶ Don't interrupt.

▶ Speak clearly so everyone can hear you.

17

PART TWO

Study Skills & Language Skills

CONTENTS

Study Skills

Dictionary 20

Parts of a Book 21

Calendar 22

Telephone Directory 23

Directions 24

Lists 25

Diagrams 26

Charts and Graphs 27

Maps 28

Schedules 29

Labels 30

Messages 31

Language Skills

Punctuation Guide 32

Capitalization Guide 34

Spelling and Vocabulary 35

STUDY SKILLS

DICTIONARY

The **dictionary** tells the meanings of words. All the words are listed in **ABC order.** That means they follow the same order as the alphabet.

Many dictionaries have **guide words** at the top of each page. These tell the first and last words on the page. That helps you find your word faster.

P

puppy

A puppy is a young dog.

PARTS OF A BOOK

Grab your favorite book. What is it called? The **title** tells you. The title is the name of the book.

What else can you read on the cover? The name of the **author** is there—the person who wrote the book.

Some books have a **table of contents** up front. This is a list of what is in the book. It tells you where to find things in the book. Many books have **chapters**. These are sections of the book.

CHECK it OUT!

✔ *Look at the table of contents in this book. Choose a topic and then use the page number to find it in the book.*

CALENDAR

Well, you are all dressed. You're ready for school, but no one else is awake. Is today Saturday? A **calendar** can help you find out.

Calendars show the days of the week. They also show the date of each day. A calendar will also show which days are holidays.

Some calendars show one day at a time. Some show one month at a time. Some calendars even show the whole year at a time!

You can write on many calendars. This is a good way to remember special information.

TELEPHONE DIRECTORY

The **telephone directory** has the names of people in your community. The names are listed in ABC order. Next to each name is the address and telephone number of the person.

keep in mind
911 *is for emergencies* only!

You can find the names and phone numbers of businesses in your town. The telephone directory also has numbers for the police and fire departments.

DIRECTIONS

You are walking to the library by yourself for the first time. Do you know how to get there? Be sure you have the correct directions.

Directions tell you how to get from one place to another. The steps should always be in the proper order, from first to last.

When you give directions, a map or drawing can be helpful.

Find out about street names and abbreviations on page 34.

LISTS

You have many things to buy today. How will you remember everything? A **list** is an easy way to organize information.

When you make a list, write one item under another. This makes it easy to find the information.

You can write a list in ABC order, in number order, or in time order—any order that makes sense to you.

eggs
cereal
milk
grapes

flour
bread
turkey
yogurt
Swiss cheese

Keep a list of ideas in your journal. Add to it when you get a great idea.

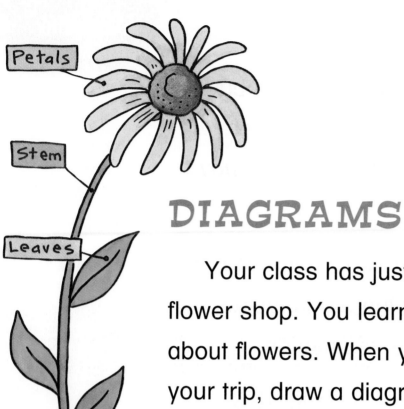

Petals

Stem

Leaves

DIAGRAMS

Your class has just visited a flower shop. You learned a lot about flowers. When you talk about your trip, draw a diagram to help you remember what you learned.

A **diagram** is a picture that shows all the parts of something. The **labels** on a diagram tell you the name of each part. A diagram can help make information easier to understand. When you draw a diagram, be sure all the labels are in the right places.

PSST!

A diagram shows how something works, too.

CHARTS AND GRAPHS

How many of your friends like pizza? How many like hot dogs?

A **chart** is a way to show information. Charts are usually organized in columns.

A **graph** is another way to show information. Graphs can use bars or even pictures to give information.

CHECK it OUT!

✔ *Look at a report you wrote. Would a chart or a graph help?*

27

MAPS

Read about maps and directions on page 24.

Where does the bus go? Will it stop near Grandma's house?

A **map** could tell you the answers. Some maps show just one neighborhood. Other maps show the whole country or the whole world.

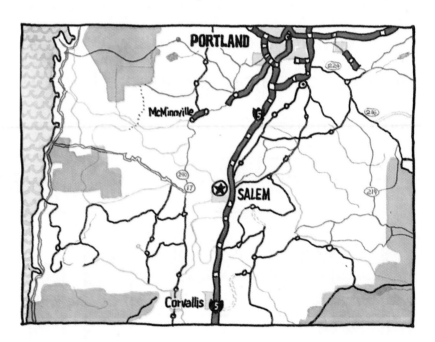

Maps tell you which way to go. They also show how far one place is from another.

SCHEDULES

Are you going on a train trip? You have your ticket. How will you know what time the train leaves?

A **schedule** will tell you when the train leaves. It will also show when you will get to your stop. A schedule shows what time something will happen.

There are schedules for trains, buses, and airplanes. You can make a schedule. It can help you arrange times for your chores.

keep in mind

Remember to check if the time on a schedule is A.M. or P.M.!

WESTPORT TO NEW YORK

MONDAY TO FRIDAY, EXCEPT HOLIDAYS

Leave	Arrive	Leave	Arrive
New York	Westport	Westport	New York
AM	**AM**	**AM**	**PM**
5:33	6:38	11:26	12:29
6:05	7:10	11:34	12:38
6:21	7:18	12:34	1:38
6:39	7:41	1:34	2:38
6:54	7:57	2:34	3:38
7:21	8:28	3:34	4:38
7:27	8:44	4:32	5:46
7:53	8:57	5:35	6:46
8:11	9:20	6:35	7:44
8:23	9:22	7:34	8:38
8:59	10:00	8:34	9:38
9:35	10:38	9:34	10:38
10:26	11:29	10:34	11:38
10:34	11:38	11:59	1:03
11:05	12:09	12:29	2:01

SATURDAY, SUNDAY & HOLIDAYS

AM	**AM**	**PM**	**PM**
1:23	2:28	3:34	4:38
5:32	6:40	4:34	5:38
6:35	7:40	5:34	6:38
7:35	8:40	6:23	7:22
8:23	9:22	6:34	7:36
8:34	9:38	7:23	8:22
9:23	10:22	7:34	8:38

LABELS

keep in mind

The first ingredient on a food label is the most important one. That's what the food has most of.

Stores have so many things to choose from. It's hard to know what to buy. **Labels** can help you decide.

Labels are important. A clothing label tells what the fabric is made of. It also tells how to wash the clothing.

A food label lists ingredients. It also tells where the product was made.

Reading labels can help make you a better shopper.

FROM THE KITCHEN

10:30 A.M.
Mom, Aunt Paula
called. She will be
here at 11:00.

Jason

MESSAGES

The phone is ringing! If it's not for you, you should take a message. A **message** is a short note that tells who the caller was and what he or she wanted. It should also tell what time the person called.

When you give a message, say your name clearly, so the person you wanted will know who called.

CHECK it OUT!

When you take a message, sign your name, too. Then the person will know who wrote the information.

LANGUAGE SKILLS

PUNCTUATION GUIDE

End Punctuation

Use a **period** at the end of a statement.

Jan rides a blue bike.

Use a **question mark** at the end of a question.

Where is the dog?

Use an **exclamation mark** at the end of a sentence that shows strong feeling.

I hit a home run!

Commas

Use a **comma** between the name of a city and a state in an address.

Oklahoma City, Oklahoma

Use a **comma** between the day and year in a date.

August 24, 1959

Use a **comma** after the greeting in a friendly letter and after the closing in all letters.

Dear Jamie,   Best wishes,

Quotation Marks

Use **quotation marks** before and after a direct quotation, the exact words that a speaker says.

Darlene said, "I'll be back later."

CAPITALIZATION GUIDE

Capitalize the first word of a sentence.

My friend eats an apple.

Capitalize all words in a letter's greeting.

Dear Danny,

Capitalize the first word in the closing of a letter.

Yours truly,

Abbreviations

Some words can be written in a shorter form. The shorter form starts with a capital letter and ends with a period.

Street–St. Doctor–Dr. Mister–Mr.

SPELLING AND VOCABULARY

Sounding out words can help you spell them. Try these steps:

▶ Say the word to yourself.

▶ Listen to the sounds.

▶ Then try to spell the word.

▶ Use a dictionary to check your spelling.

Correct spelling makes your writing easier to read. Your readers will like that!

Here are some spelling tips for you.

▶ Add *s* to most nouns to make them name more than one thing.

dog/dogs	cat/cats
toe/toes	ear/ears

▶ If a noun ends in *ch, s, ss, sh, x,* or *z,* add *es* to name more than one thing.

inch/inches	dish/dishes
buzz/buzzes	ax/axes

▶ Some words aren't said the same way they are spelled.

said	light	neighbor
says	cough	friend
been	sign	Wednesday

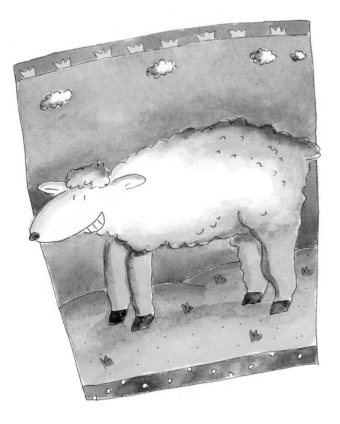

▶ Some words have silent letters.
Here are some tricky words you
should remember.

silent b: climb   lamb   crumb

silent h: ghost   rhyme

silent k: knee   knot

silent l: talk   walk   half

silent w: two   whole   write

Writing Models

CONTENTS

Descriptive Writing 40

Narrative Writing 42

Informative Writing 44

Expository Writing 46

DESCRIPTIVE WRITING

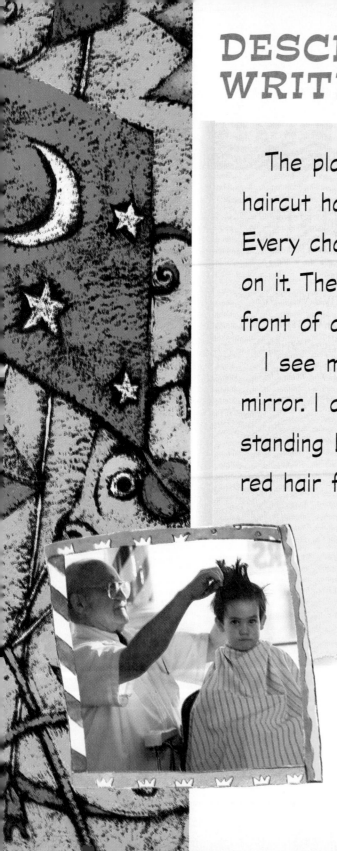

The place I go to for a haircut has three green chairs. Every chair has a blue towel on it. There is a big mirror in front of all the chairs.

I see myself in the big mirror. I can see the barber standing behind me. I see my red hair falling to the floor. I don't see the hair falling down my neck. But I feel it!

✔ *Do your descriptions tell about things in a certain order?*

There is a special picture in my house. It is a picture of my uncle and me at a picnic. In the back is the tree that we climbed. At one side of the picture is the picnic table. At the other side is the lake. We went swimming there. Right in the middle is Uncle Rafael giving me a big hug. That's my favorite part of the picture!

NARRATIVE WRITING

keep in mind

You can write stories about real things. You can write stories about things you make up.

My dad and I were riding on the bus. It seemed like a really long ride. I looked out the window. There were lots of store signs. First, I saw a shoe store. Then, I saw a dress shop and a pizza restaurant. At last, I saw my favorite store. It was my grandpa's bookstore. That's where we got off. Hooray!

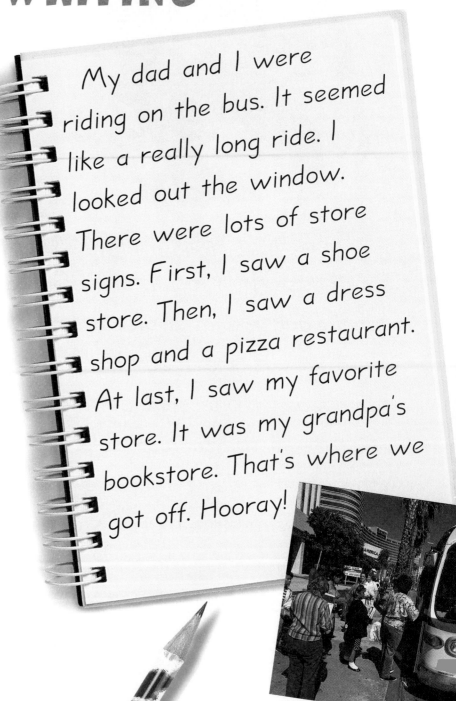

April 11, 1998

Dear Jean,

On our trip to the city, I saw a clown in the street. She had a pet parrot that sang and told jokes. They both made me laugh. It was a lot of fun. Maybe next time you can come with us. I hope you can.

Your friend,
Tyrone

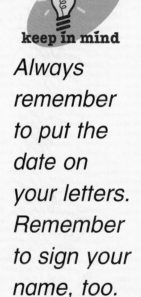

keep in mind

Always remember to put the date on your letters. Remember to sign your name, too.

INFORMATIVE WRITING

4 o'clock

Hi, Mom!

I am at Amy's house. We are playing with her new kittens. Her mother said it was okay. I will call you later.

Donna

PSST!

A note is one way to share information quickly.

Snakes are very interesting. Their skin is dry and smooth. They use their tongues to test the air. Some snakes live in trees. Other snakes live under rocks in the desert. Sometimes they can travel very fast! The zoo is a good place to learn more about snakes.

keep in mind

Remember to give details when you write a report.

EXPOSITORY WRITING

PSST!

Before you follow directions, be sure you know right and left.

I walk to school with my big brother. We leave the house and walk down Elm Street. We walk one block to Main Street. We turn left. We walk to Oak Avenue. We turn right. We walk one block to Taylor Lane. There's my school, straight ahead!

How We Fly a Kite

First, I wait for a windy day. Then I go to the park with my sister. We climb to the top of the hill, and my sister holds the kite. Next, I start to run down the hill. Then I let out the string on my kite. When the string gets long, my sister lets go. At last, the wind catches the kite and it goes up into the sky.

CHECK it OUT!

✔ Look at directions you wrote. Are the steps in the right order?

47

Illustration
Part 1: Michele Noiset 4-5, 9a (strip), 13a (strip), 14a (strip), 16a (strip); Bonnie Matthews 7, 8, 12a, 12b; Dick Codor 9 (spot), 11a, 11b; Ken Bowser 10; Patrick Merrell 13; Nadine Westcott 14-15; Elliot Kreloff 16, 17. **Part 2:** Kimble Pendleton Mead 18-19, 20a (strip), 32 (strip), 35 (strip); Dick Codor 20, 23a,b,c, 25, 28, 29a,b; Ken Bowser 21, 24; Patrick Merrell 22, 26, 27; Bonnie Matthews 30, 31, 33, 34, 36, 37a, 37b. **Part 3:** Daphne McCormack 38-39, 40 (strip); Bonnie Matthews 47; Dick Codor 44.

Photography
All photographs are by the Macmillan/McGraw-Hill School Division (MMSD) except as noted below.

Part 3: Nancy Brown/Image Bank 41; Phil McCarten/PhotoEdit 42; Gary Buss/FPG International 46L; Roy Morsch/The Stock Market 46M; Sotographs/The Stock Market 46R.

Design and Production by BB&K Design Inc.